NOW YOU CAN READ ABOUT...
REPTILES

TEXT BY HARRY STANTON

ILLUSTRATED BY PHIL WEARE

BRIMAX BOOKS • NEWMARKET • ENGLAND

Crocodiles and lizards are reptiles. So are snakes and turtles. A tortoise is also a reptile—have you got one as a pet?

Look at these pictures.
Do you know what these
reptiles are called?

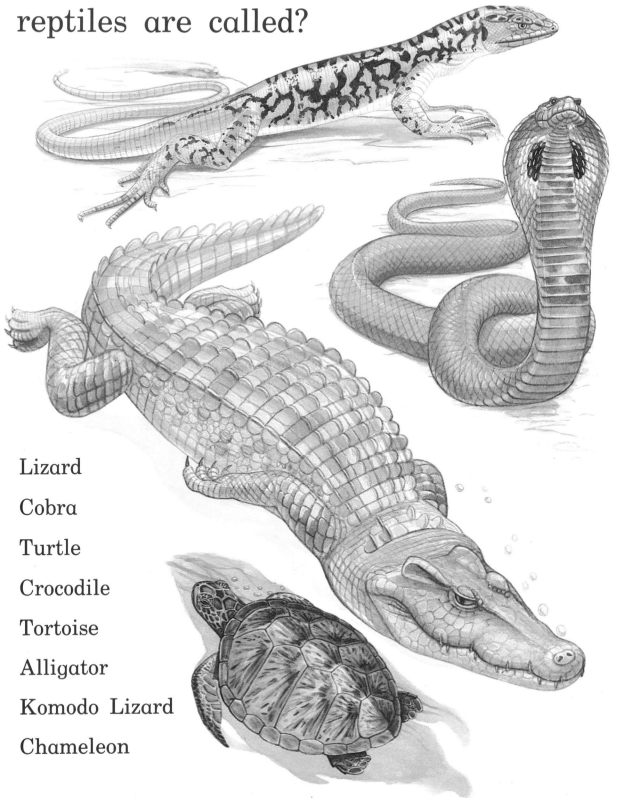

Lizard

Cobra

Turtle

Crocodile

Tortoise

Alligator

Komodo Lizard

Chameleon

Most chameleons live in trees. Their feet and tails can easily grip the branches. They move very little and hide by changing their colour.

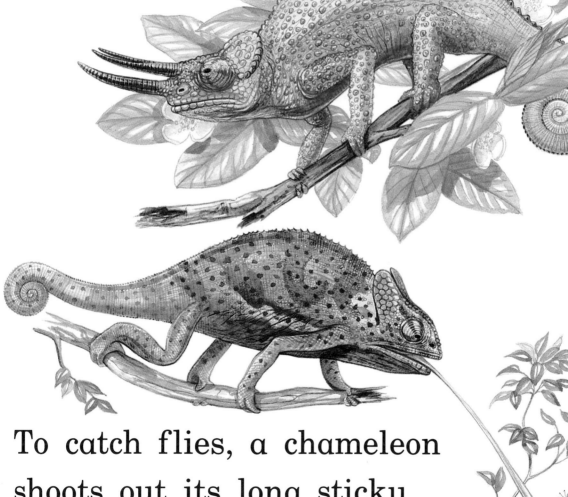

To catch flies, a chameleon shoots out its long sticky tongue. This tongue may be almost as long as the chameleon.

The anaconda is the largest snake in the world. It is as long as a bus or a coach. It kills its prey by squeezing it.

Rattlesnakes are found in America. They make a sound like a baby's rattle, to warn other creatures to keep away.

Swimming in the river is a red-bellied water snake.

Here is a grass snake. Grass snakes like to live in damp places. They are good swimmers. They cannot harm you.

The cobra is a poisonous snake. This snake is found in Africa.

There are nearly three thousand different kinds of snakes. Very few of them are poisonous. Many are harmless. Some snakes kill their prey by coiling round it and squeezing hard. Others catch their prey in their jaws. They swallow it whole.

The smallest lizards
may only be a few
centimetres long.
Largest of all are
the Komodo Dragons.
These live on islands
in the Pacific Ocean.
They can grow to over
three metres in length.

Lizards can be found in all parts of the world. Some live in trees. Some live in deserts. Many of them burrow underground. A few can even glide from tree to tree.

The female covers the eggs with sand. The heat of the sun helps to hatch the eggs. Sixty days later baby turtles scramble down the beach to the sea.

Sea Turtles live in the ocean. The males seldom go ashore. The females only go ashore to lay their eggs. They dig holes in sandy beaches, in which to lay their eggs.

On the Galapagos Islands in the Pacific Ocean are the biggest and oldest tortoises in the world. The giant tortoise is so large that a man can ride on its back. The oldest is over one hundred and fifty years of age.

There are over two hundred different kinds of tortoise.

Some of them live on land, some live in water. They move very slowly. They are able to hide from their enemies by pulling their head, legs and tail into their thick shells.

They also lie in wait with only their eyes and noses above the water.
They are ready for any animals and birds that may come down to the water's edge for a drink.

Alligators and crocodiles
eat fish, snails and crabs
they find in the water.
Crocodiles lay up to sixty
eggs in a mud lined nest.
The mother guards the nest
until they hatch.
The babies have to find their
own food, but the mother will
guard them for a week or two.

Crocodiles have heavy bodies
and short strong legs. They
can walk and even run on land.
With the help of a strong tail
and webbed feet, they are very
good swimmers.

Crocodiles and alligators live in warm rivers. They can grow very big. Some are over six metres long.

In the colder parts of the world snakes, lizards and tortoises may sleep during the winter. They hide in a warm, dry place until spring.

Reptiles have dry skins covered in some form of scales. As they are cold blooded, they do not sweat. To become warmer reptiles lie in the sun. To become cooler, they hide in the shade.

There are over six thousand
different kinds of reptiles.
They can be very different
in shape. Some of them live
on land. Some of them live
in water and some even live
in trees.